Israel
Redeemed
Rabbi Meir Kahane's last speech

ZE'EV SHEMER

ISBN: 1491005416
ISBN-13: 978-1491005415

DEDICATION

To honor the memory of Rabbi Meir Kahane z"tl and his son Rabbi Binyamin Ze'ev Kahane z"tl who were murdered in cold blood by Muslim terrorists. They were a testament to *mesirut nefesh* (self-sacrifice) and truc scholar-warriors who will forever be a light onto all who continue to strive to bring about Israel's redemption.

ZE'EV SHEMER

CONTENTS

ZE'EV SHEMER

ACKNOWLEDGMENTS

I want to thank the hill top youth and the valiant Jewish settlers who spent countless hours with me sharing their stories and memories. A special thanks to those that left the shadows of exile and made their way back to our ancestral land; and especially to those who continue to follow in the footsteps of Rav Meir Kahane and other true scholar-warriors like him. Thank you to all who dare.

ISRAEL REDEEMED

Rabbi Meir Kahane's famous address to the National Press Club was given a short while after he received one seat in the Israeli Knesset in 1984. He gave a similar speech in New York the night he was murdered, with the added emphasis on the need of every Jew to return to his homeland. Note that this speech was given before the Oslo Accords were signed and before the Palestinian Liberation Organization (PLO) received land and weapons and became known as the Palestinian Autonomy. It was before suicide-bombings, the Intifada (Arab uprising), and 15 years before the attacks of 9-11. His accurate predictions made him a controversial political figure. Two decades later, his proposed solution to the Arab-Israeli conflict seems more relevant than ever.

Rabbi Kahane speaks:

"They hated him in the gates he who rebukes, and they abhorred he who speaks the truth" a verse from the book of Amos[1].

In 1938 Ze'ev Jabotinsky visited Vilna and the leftists in Vilna particularly the Socialist Bundt, put out a leaflet, which they handed out to the Jews of Vilna. I want to read it to you. Ze'ev Jabotinsky of course was the greatest of the Zionist leaders of his time and in 1938 he was appealing to the Jews of Poland and Europe to escape, to run, to leave before tragedy struck them. And the Bundt issued the following leaflet, which has been translated from Yiddish into English:

---

[1] Amos was one of the Biblical prophets in the *Tanach* who forewarned the Jewish people of the upcoming Roman siege.

"To the Jewish workers and the Jewish masses of Vilna, the spiritual father of Jewish fascism, the paper general Jabotinsky is coming to Vilna. Of late this adventurer and charlatan has become very popular with the Jewish workers and Jewish masses of Vilna; show your contempt for the Purim general and give him this command: Get out! Evacuate yourself along with your friends from Poland. Down with Fascism, Down with Jabotinsky."

When I read this particular leaflet, it reminded me of the truth that nothing ever changes. Nothing ever changes! The Jewish people learn nothing from history, repeat the same tragedies. I cannot begin to tell you, the hate, the sheer psychopathic hate, which is raging today in the state of Israel. Not against Arafat and not against the PLO, and not against Syria but against Jews!

They have created a new label in Israel called "Kahanism", and I want you to know what Kahanism is, Kahanism is a label and an outlet for vicious hatred against Judaism. And those who march against Kahanism tomorrow will march to trample on Judaism.

In Givatayim, a suburb of Tel Aviv 10,000 leftists came from all over the country. Bused in from the Kibbutzim, they came with iron bars, they came with stones, they attacked Jews, they beat Jews. The Mayor of Givatayim, a member of the Marach (Labor party), stood and shouted "laarog otam kaasher hem ktanim!" - kill them while they are still small! This is the face of the left in Israel. And as I watched that crowd, the twisted faces, the obscenities, the curses, I said to myself, now I understand what happened in Israel 40 years ago, at the time of the "HaSidon" - The Season. And everyone must know what happened in those days.

It is those that don't know what happened in the past that will live to see it happen again in the present and in the future.

In the 1940's these same Kibbutznikim, HaShomer HaTzair, Meretz, Labor, the same liberal Jews that today speak about democracy, and love of all the people, they speak about ethics, and morality... they kidnapped Jewish soldiers of the Irgun and the Sternist Jewish fighters, and they turned them over to the British, knowing that to be a member of the Irgun was a capital punishment, a death sentence.

They were the ones who in 1948 fired upon the Irgun ship, the Altalena (a ship that was smuggling weapons for the Jewish fighters to use against the British and Arab militants) and murdered in cold blood 17 Jews because Menachem Begin was on the ship and they wanted to liquidate Begin[2]. And know who the commander of the operation was, his name was Yitzhak Rabin. He gave the order to fire and to murder 17 Jews. And know that the next day in the Knesset, the Prime Minister at that time, Ben Gurion, rose and in the minutes he said, "blessed be the holy canon", blessed be the holy canon that murdered seventeen Jews!

---

[2] Menachem Begin was a right-wing Jewish leader who later on became Prime Minister of Israel

They speak to us about Democracy and about love? They were the ones who murdered in cold blood in the 1920's one of the leaders of Agudat Israel, Yaakov Yisrael Dahan, because he was an anti-Zionist. So you can oppose an anti- Zionist, but to murder a Jew in cold blood? And know who gave the orders: Yitzhak Ben Zvi, the second President of the State of Israel.

They speak about Fascism? About hooligans? They turn now to the Sephardic Jews and tell them to watch out for Kahane! They turn to Sephardic Jews? The leftists? How ironic! Because I remember what they did! How they destroyed whole communities of Jews from Morocco, and Algeria and Libya, and Tunisia and Egypt, and Syria and Iraq and Yemen!

In the 1940's as the State came into being, hundreds of thousands of Jews poured in from Arab countries. Every one of those Jews was a Zionist, a real Zionist, not the Herzl type of Zionist! They were Zionists for 2000 years, "ve techezena enenu leTzion" - may our eyes behold the return to Zion. That was real Zionism.

They were warm Jews, religious Jews, and what happened to them! The leftists from Mapai and Mapam stood and watched as 800,000 Jews poured into the country, and they asked themselves the only question that had any meaning to them, the only thing that bothered them, the thing that meant more to them than the State, than the Jewish people, the question was: "For whom will they vote?" They saw they were all religious Jews, "they will not vote for us" they thought, so they went about purposely in cold blood, to spiritually destroy an entire people.

Jews were put into 'mabarot,' transit camps, and if there was a job, they asked you "in what school have you registered your child?" and if it was a religious school, there was no job! And they would say, "take this paper and take it to the Histadrut School (Labor Union), register your child in a Histadrut school; the Principal will then stamp the paper and you will bring it to the Labor Exchange office and you will get a job". If you wanted a job they would ask, "where is your red book of the Histadrut? You are not a member? No job!"

Fascism? I know who the Fascists were and who the Fascists are! The pity is that we waited 37 years to put someone in the Knesset to give to them, just as they gave to us! I have arrived!!

They speak of "kfiat dati" - religious coercion. Llet me speak to you about religious coercion. In 1948 10,000 Yemenite boys, children, came to Israel without their parents under the auspices of Youth Aliyah. Every Yemenite boy that came to Israel, came with his Shabbat, with his Kashrut, and with his "Simanim", that's what they called the "peyott" - the ear-locks that every Yemenite boy had. The Simanim, the sign of the Jew. For 2000 years they had the Simanim, for 2000 years they had the Shabbat, for 2000 years they suffered but remained Jewish, then they came to the Holy Land to places as 'holy' as the Kibbutzim of the Shomer HaTzair[3]. They ripped from them their Simanim, their Judaism, their Jewishness, children ages 7, 8 and 9.

---

[3] Youth movement for the non-religious liberal new-Zionists.

Shimon Peres speaks today about the tragedy that there is crime in Israel. Crime in Israel? "Boker Tov" - good morning! If there is crime in Israel, who created it? If there are gangs in Israel, who created them? And if there is a breakdown in everything that is Jewish in Israel, who created that? If not Shimon Peres and his gangsters?! They ripped from Jews the only values they had, their Judaism, and left them naked to pick up the values of Dizengoff Street[4]; and now they complain about hoodlums and gangsters.

---

[4] Dizengoff Street is in the heart of Tel Aviv, known for its nightlife, commerce and unfortunately an abundance of drugs and prostitution.

I sat in prison in Israel; I saw the Yemenites, the Iraqis, and the Moroccans, who never knew what crime was when they lived in Morocco and Yemen and Iraq. They never tasted it, they came to Israel and were destroyed spirituality by people who cynically cared only about "for whom will they vote?" So when I say these things in the 'Kikar' - in the town square, of course the people listen and of course people clap, and of course people cheer because finally someone is coming and saying the truth, he is saying what they have always thought all these years.

You think it's an accident that so many people are shouting 'Kahane'? It's not an accident. I touched upon the things that bother them, that trouble them, the things that no one else is saying to them. I want a Jewish State. I don't want a Hebrew speaking copy of Time Square!

I want to give to those people, the Sephardic Jews that came to Israel with 'Kavod' - honor, self respect, the respect for the family, respect for their father, their mother, they came with respect and honor; and it was taken from them, and they were told, your father is a 'primitivi' - a primitive; and your mother is a 'primitivit' - she is primitive, "she is backwards"; Backwards?

They who raised their children with honor and pride, to work and not to steal, they were primitive? It is the European, the Hellenism, this Western Hellenized culture, which first destroyed the Jews of the West and now they use it to wipe out the Jews from Arab countries. That will not be. I don't want a Hellenist State, I want a Jewish State and that is why they hate me so.

I want to save the Jewish soul and the Jewish body, and I want to tell you that the Jewish body is in danger every day in Israel. If I mention the name Motty Swuissa, I don't know if 10 people here know the name. But Motty Swuissa just two weeks ago was murdered. He was murdered in Israel; not in Lebanon and not in the 'Occupied Territories ' of Yossi Sarid. He was murdered near Beit Shemesh, 20 kilometers from Yerushalayim he and his fiancé were murdered in cold blood by Arabs.

The same day another Jew was murdered in the north, in Migdal HaEmek. This is a pattern now; they are killing Jews in Israel every single week. Who cares? What is the answer? We came to Israel to die? We came to Israel to live. Today for the first time Jews in Israel are frightened, Jews are afraid in Israel. It's becoming Brooklyn.

A Jewish woman comes to me in Kiriyat Atta, a suburb of Haifa, and tells me "I'm afraid to let my child play in the streets." This is the dream of Zion? For this we waited 2000 years? Soldiers are afraid.

Shaltiel Akiva, -there aren't five people here who remember that name- a 21 year-old soldier from the Yemenite town of Rosh Ayin, who spent eight months in Lebanon without a scratch, he came back safely. The night he returned he was murdered. And his father told me the story after the funeral the next day; he said the previous evening his son Shaltiel, phoned and said, "I'm at the 'trempiada'" -the hitch-hikers' stop- five kilometers away from Rosh Ayin. For those that don't know, Rosh Ayin is near Petach Tikvah in the heart of Israel. "I am five kilometers away from home please prepare supper for me" so they prepared supper for him and they waited 15 minutes, and half-an-hour, and an hour, they waited all night and he never arrived. The next day they brought his body. Shaltiel had been murdered by Arabs inside the State of Israel while hitching a ride!

Moshe Tamam, -that name virtually nobody remembers- was a 19 year-old soldier hitching a ride near Netanya. Arabs picked him up and gave him a ride. They found his body four days later. And know what they did to him so you know whom we are dealing with. They gouged out his eyes, and they cut off his sexual organs; and that is what we are dealing with. And of such people our Rabbis told us already, and the Humash[5] told us already, "Ishmael will be a wild man, his hand will be against everybody and everybody's hand will be against him." That's with whom we're dealing! This is the enemy. This is Ishmael.

My son came home from the army, he came from Miluim (reserve duty) and he showed me a letter, which was given to every soldier; a letter from the Israeli Defense Forces. "Let me see the letter, let me see pride I told him." Do you know what the letter said? It said,

---

[5] The Torah or Jewish Bible also referred to as the Five Books of Moses.

"Hayal -soldier- be careful when hitching rides". Soldier of Israel be careful on the roads of Israel, you might be killed by Arabs in Israel! What a tragedy, what a disgrace, what a Hilul HaShem! (Desecration of God's name). But [according to liberals] the enemy is Kahanism?

All of this doesn't bother the enemies of Kahanism, but it bothers me. That Jews who came after 2000 years in the exile, are assimilating inside Israel. When you visit Israel you are tourists, you don't see anything. You see the Wall, you see Masada, and the Plaza Hotel; you don't see the tragedy that occurs not far from the Plaza and on every town and every city.

The Arabs come into the towns, to meet Jewish girls. In the morning the Arab wakes up in his village and he is Ibrahim, he comes to Jerusalem or Netanya and suddenly his name is Avi, "Hello, my name is Avi." There are over 3500 Jewish women married to Arabs and over 10,000 Jewish women living with Arabs in Israel. In Beit Shemesh I'll never forget the Jew that came over to me, a man in his 50's and said to me, "Rav Kahane," he said, "I have two daughters and they are both married to Arabs. One lives in the Arab village of Taiba." and then he said, "When I lived in Morocco did I ever dream in my blackest nightmare, that my daughter would ever go out with an Arab? In Morocco? Never heard of such a thing! We came to the Holy Land and my daughters married Arabs!"

That doesn't bother anybody?

The President of Israel *"hometz ben yain"* - vinegar the son of wine, the son of the chief Rabbi, this Helenist goes to visit Nevey Shalom, a settlement founded by a Jew who converted to Christianity and is now a monk; a settlement where Jews and Arabs live together, and he says *"ze keren ohr"* - this is a ray of light. This is our

President? This is our president!

On the beaches of Israel in the summer time, you see cars parked, most with license plates from Shechem, Jenin, Tulkarm, Hevron, Aza, what are they looking for? Sun and water? There is sun and water in Aza (Gaza) too. They are looking for Jewish women! The prostitutes in Israel are all Jewish, the pimps are mostly Arabs and we, we bare the shame, because this is not new, this has been going on for 30 years. When did you last hear the religious (political) parties in Israel, let alone the other parties, speak up about this? The irony, it would laughable; it would be a joke out of Chelm if it weren't so tragic.

The religious head of the Druze, Sheik Taari, appealed to the chief Rabbi of Haifa to come out and oppose intermarriage of Druze men with Jewish women. So when you saw in the paper that the chief Rabbi of Haifa came out... no! After 20 years he came out because the Druze asked him too.

In Haifa they have, a center called Beit HaGefen. It is funded by the city of Haifa with public funds. It is a center for assimilation, intermarriage and the destruction of Jewish values. Jewish women and Arab men, and it is always Jewish women because an Arab woman is not allowed to go out of her village, let alone to go out with a Jew. The Arab goes into Haifa and there's no problem, he isn't afraid; but let an Israeli Jew go into an Arab village any evening to look for an Arab woman, they'll slice him into little pieces. Who speaks of these things? Who talks of this? This tragedy that is taking place today in Israel?

And above all, the tragedy of the gradual and not so gradual birthrate of the Arabs in Israel. Because we are such foolish people and unwise, we pay them for each baby, each month a check from 'bituach leumi'-National Insurance. For one baby, one check, two babies, two checks; ten babies? Here, take a book of checks! Every month! You want a tourist site? I'll give you a tourist site no tour guide would ever take you to: On the twentieth of every month go to the main post office, in every major city and watch the hundreds of Arabs in line waiting to cash their checks. And count how many checks each one of them has. 10 checks, 15 checks, 18 checks, why not? The Galilee today has a majority of Arabs. Today! Not in twenty years, but today!

Jews are afraid at night to drive through Arab villages in the Galilee, so they are building access roads to go around so God forbid we shouldn't have to drive through them. Entire cities in Israel are becoming Arab. Jaffa is becoming Arab, Ramle is becoming Arab, Lod, Akko, Nazareth Ilit built by the Israeli government to meet the Arab Nazareth is today 25% Arab.

Why? Arabs come with dollars, and they offer twice the price for the apartment in cash. And where does this money come from? It is PLO money and comes across Jordan; and it comes across freely and the government knows about it. They are quiet about it and they say, "It doesn't hurt anyone, the important thing is they are quiet, and after all it's a Democracy" (sic).

They are buying Jewish land and we are committing suicide.

I however, am not ready to commit suicide in the name of Democracy. For 40 years we have been *'frayerim'* – fools; but I am not a fool, I will not sit quietly. I don't hate Arabs. I love Jews! And I hate the enemies of the Jews, not because they are Arabs but because they are enemies! You think there is a single Arab living in Israel in a place that is called the Jewish State?

Liberals have immense contempt for the Arabs; they believe that they can buy them. "We'll raise their living standards and then they'll be good Arabs" Good Arabs? What contempt! They think that a good Arab is one that will agree to the Jews living in what he considers to be his Palestine.

You think there is one Arab who enjoys living in a State where there is a law of return that applies to Jews and not to non-Jews? You think there is one Arab who enjoys living in a State, which has a National Anthem – Hatikvah- with words that say *'nefesh yehudi omia'* - the soul of the Jew yearns? You can imagine how that sits with them. You think there is one Arab who enjoys living in a State whose Independence Day celebrates his defeat? You can't buy a person by giving him an indoor toilet. "You see, you had no toilet, now you have one." You can't come and say as the UJA says: "What do you want? We came and we turned the desert into a garden" Let me tell you what the Arab says: "Yes it's true, but it was my desert and now it's your garden." I respect the Arab, and that is why he has to go!

Because I know you can't buy him, you can't buy his national pride; know that he hates the Jews and that if we allowed them they would do to us what Arabs do to other Arabs today in Lebanon, and Syria, and Egypt. They would do to us what they did to us yesterday. Do you know what Arabs did to us in the 1920's and 1930's? Do you know what they did to us? When there was no Kahane, no Begin and no other 'fascists'? Do you know what they did to us when there was no State of Israel? What they did in Hevron and in Jaffa, and Yerushalaym? How they murdered over 500 Jews?![6] They would do that to us if we let them, but I am not going to let them!

---

[6] This is an historical reference to the massacre of Jews by Arabs in 1929 (18 years before the re-establishment of the Jewish State).

I want an exchange of populations. Beginning in 1948 we took in 800,000 Jews from Arab countries; that was phase one. Now I want phase two: We took Jews from Arab countries? Well now we'll give them Arabs from the Jewish country!

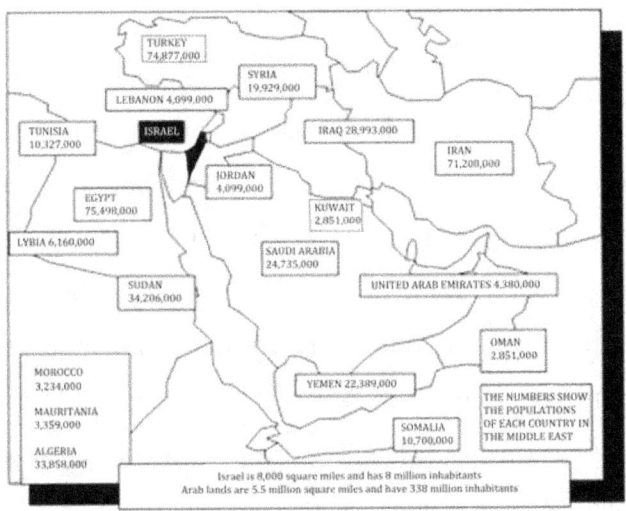

I am ready to offer the Arabs that want to leave voluntarily compensation for their properties, which is more that what they did for the Jews they expelled from Morocco, from Egypt, from Iraq. Do you know how much money Jews in those countries left behind? Billions of dollars, and they were never compensated for it. And when we signed the treaty with Egypt we didn't even have the decency, the self-respect to demand compensation for the properties seized by Gamal Abdel Nasser from the Jews in Egypt. I am better than they; I will give compensation to the Arabs that are willing to leave. And those that are not willing to leave, I will throw out without monetary compensation!

This is racism? My God, this is saving ourselves; this is self-preservation! I don't hate the Arabs, I wish them well, elsewhere! I wish them the very best in any of their 22 countries. I have only one, it is mine and I am not going to lose it to either Bush or Begin. We can't continue in this way. We cannot continue as the country rapidly becomes more Arab, not in 40 years, not in 30, in 10 the Arabs will help the leftists become a majority in the Knesset, a coalition of Yossi Sarid, Shimon Peres, Mr. Shemtov and the Arabs, that will be the coalition if we don't do anything about this.

I am appalled by Jews who say, "This is what the Germans did to the Jews." Did the Jews of Germany ever say, "Germany is our country and the Germans stole it from us? And when we become the majority we will take it back and call it Israel?" That is not what they said. The Jews of Germany wanted nothing more than to be the best Germans that ever lived. The Arabs don't want to be Israelis.

Let everyone know that when we came out to oppose the Camp David Accords and peace treaty with Egypt, they said "Kahane doesn't want peace", I want peace, but I knew what kind of peace we would have with Egypt. Peace? Any country with a modicum of self-respect would have recalled their ambassador from Egypt. If Egypt had done to them what they did to us: murdered in cold blood seven Jews. I don't know if any of you know what the real story is, I am sure that it came here to you as "one crazy Arab shoots..." and every time an Arab shoots, he's crazy.

So the story came as 'one crazy Arab soldier shot Jews and also wounded his own soldiers', well that's a lie!

Another Egyptian lie. A typical Arab lie.

He wasn't crazy, he was a member of the Muslim Brotherhood and other soldiers stood by and watched him shoot, and three of our seven soldiers did not die right away, they laid there bleeding, and the Egyptians refused to allow medical aid. And those three soldiers bled to death. And Mubarak said, "Why should a little incident upset our relationship?" A little incident? If I would have been Prime Minister I would have given him a little incident!

I am tired. I'm tired of going to funerals, I didn't come to Israel to go to funerals; I came to Israel for *'smachot'* - happy occasions, joy, and happiness. There is a growing fear in Israel and you can tell by the hysteria, the hysterical obsession with Kahanism. President Herzog is obsessed with Kahane, he goes to bed every night with 'Kahane'. Shimon Peres says Kahane is the greatest danger to Israel, I would have imagined that Syria would be, but no.

The army radio station Galey Tzahal, devoted last week 18 hours, an entire day to Kahane, to attacks on Kahane the army radio station! An army that is supposed to be above politics, being crudely used by politicians and do you know why? Because they are terrified, because they know that as much as they are against Kahane, in the streets, the people of Israel are for Kahane!

It's not an accident that the Sephardic Jews in Israel are

for Kahane, why? Because they did not learn about Arabs in a seminar at Hebrew University, they learned about Arabs because they lived under Arabs. So naturally when Kahane says what he says; they say "kol hakavod" - with all the honor, (meaning -you're absolutely right), because I say what they think. And the young people they are with us and that's what terrifies the Labor and the Likud. Yes the Likud. Pains me more than anything to have to tell you that the Likud has joined actively with the leftists in physically breaking up rallies of the Kach movement.

It's not to be believed, people who once had this thing done to them, and I remember how Menachem Begin in 1952 was prevented from speaking to the people in Afula. Leftist hoodlums broke up his rallies, and now they do the same? Do you know why? They are afraid of losing votes. They know that the people say that the Likud of today is not the Likud of yesterday. The Likud of Begin is not what it once was.

And we have to stop being idol worshipers. We do not worship idols. The Likud should be backed if it does for the people, if it doesn't we don't back it. With God's help in the next elections the latest poll in Israel shows 12 seats for us in the Knesset. And I tell you that is not true, not true! For everyone who is openly and willing to admit that he will vote Kach, there is another one who will do so quietly. I am not interested in Seats; I'm going for the whole ballgame!

I want a government of Kahane, Ariel Sharon and Raful and then you will see what we will do. Finally for those who ask: "how can you do it? How can you throw a million and a half Arabs?" I'll tell you how. Three years ago I served in the army; I was stationed near Ramallah, in Samaria, the West Bank, and the Arabs rioted in Ramallah so they sent me to put down the riots.

I want to tell you, not more than five minutes passed and the whole town heard "Kahane is here!" there was absolute silence in that town, the riots stopped. It is imperative you understand what the name Kahane means to the Arabs. For them it is a monster, it is terror, they hear Kahane and they are terrified! And that is good because that is the only language they understand.

So how will we move out the Arabs? Think for a moment. Three years from now the Arab wakes up in the morning, turns on the radio and hears in the news that Kahane is the new Prime Minister of the State of Israel. Can you imagine what he will feel? How will I move them out? There will be no need. Half will leave by themselves, the other half, will beg me, "let us go" and because I'm big about it, I'll let them go.

My friends, Israel is at a crossroads right now. The All-Mighty gave us with His kindness, His *Hessed* - mercy, He gave us a Jewish State after 2000 years, but He is not going to give us a Jewish State without us working and suffering if we're not going to make the kind of State that He wants. I want Democracy for Jews but I don't want Democracy for Arabs because otherwise there won't be a Jewish State! And for those people that say "that is not nice," you answer this question: If you are such Democrats, are you willing to allow the Arabs, peacefully, quietly, democratically to sit every night and make love not war and allow them to be the majority, quietly and peacefully? You would be shocked and amazed to know how many Jews in Israel would answer 'yes' in Israel.

We have to create in Israel a Jewish State not a State for Jews, I am sick and tired to hear the 'sabras' - (Jews born in Israel) come and say to me "I am not a Jew, I am an Israeli", I don't want to hear that again ever! I want a Jewish State and I want the public schools of Israel to teach Judaism, I want Jewish youngsters to know what is *tefillin* and what is a holyday, maybe they won't want to keep it but at the very least, give them the choice of knowing what it is being and not being Jewish.

On Wednesday I presented a motion of 'no confidence' in the Knesset because of the policy of the Ministry of Education which enforced a curriculum of meetings between Arab students and Jewish students. Mixed summer camps, Jewish children staying in Arab villages for the weekend and Arab children in Jewish towns for the weekend.

I presented a vote of 'no confidence' to the other Ministers and asked them, will you vote for a Jewish education and a Jewish State or will you vote for the coalition and for your seats and the money? You know how they voted... they voted for the coalition. That is the tragedy. I can understand a secular and leftist party but I cannot understand a religious party sitting by and watching our youngsters being destroyed, for whatever narrow reasons they may have.

There will be an election and when Peres returns from his Washington trip he will be on a coalition course with the Likud. Peres is ready to make far reaching concessions to Jordan. When he praised King Hussein as a man who wants peace, one can only recall when we liberated the Old City and found out what they had done to every synagogue. They destroyed every synagogue. And what they had done in Har HaZeitim - Mount of Olives, to the tombstones: they used them to pave roads and as latrine seats. He wants peace...

He wants many, many pieces of Israel.

The government is going to fall. Shimon Peres has worked hard this past year, he's got the strength and the Likud has fallen badly, there is going to be an election and they will try to stop us from running, with God's help that won't be because we have many answers to their intentions, we will be running.

Just as I told the people in Israel the choice in the next elections is between Kahane and Arafat; that is what the next elections will be all about. Kach or the PLO that's the choice there is no other choice! I appeal to you, save Israel, save your brothers and sisters and save yourselves, because God forbid, I would not want to be in your shoes if there is no more Israel.

I said I would end here but there is one more thing I want to tell you because it is vital. I believe that the State of Israel has to be the State for all the Jewish people and has to be the trustee of all the Jewish people. And I don't believe that there are boundaries that Israel cannot cross when Jews are in trouble.

And I want to tell you, that as anti-Semitism in this country (USA) grows, there will be a need for an Israel that will do things that you are not ready to do. And I want to tell you, that with God's help when I am Prime Minister, the State of Israel will never say that there are Israelis that are in trouble, we will always say that if there are Jews in trouble anywhere, our hand will reach out everywhere against those who hate Jews.

I will take your questions now."

Rabbi Meir Kahane was murdered November 5th, 1990 after giving a similar speech in a New York hotel where he urged American Jews to come home to Israel.

The following is an excerpt from the book[7]:

"Israel and the Palestinian nightmare"

by Ze'ev Shemer

The year is 1983 and in response to Arab terror and claims of Arab rights to the land of Israel, Rabbi Meir Kahane, an outspoken right-wing rabbi, establishes his political party Kach ("thus" in Hebrew). He is a proponent of inducing Palestinians to leave the West Bank voluntarily; if they refuse to leave, Kahane advocates expelling them. He believes Orthodox Judaism should be the official state religion, and claims that Israel has strayed away from the Jewish character it was originally intended to have.

In 1984 Rabbi Meir Kahane becomes a member of the Israeli Knesset when his party Kach gains one seat in the Parliament. Jews all across Israel, and from all walks of life, suddenly realize that Rabbi Meir Kahane's proposition of a population transfer has become more than mere rant. Kach intends to position the tiny Jewish state with a sound advantage to offer a peace treaty to

---

[7] From a chapter that focuses on the years 1983-1991

its Arab neighbors without resorting to life-endangering compromises. And although the idea of mass deportation and population transfer does not sit well with the majority of Jews -due to obvious references to deportations suffered in Russia and across Europe during the Holocaust- Arab violence is making his suggestion evermore desirable, reasonable and even necessary.

Rabbi Kahane responds to a United Nations resolution that equates Zionism with racism:

"A certain resolution on Zionism has been passed at the United Nations. In reality, it is a resolution on Judaism. It is important that a reply be given. It is important that the world know precisely what Zionism is and what the Jewish people are: It is important that the nations hear our proclamation: Listen world; I am Zionist, I am a Jew!

And listen too, Jew. Listen so that you will understand yourself who you are and what and why. For there is no escape from it even if one should be so foolish as to desire to flee the greatness and majesty of the Jewish destiny. Listen so that you will be able to stand proud and tall and know what to reply with dignity and not hesitant defensiveness. So that you will know from where you came and to where you go, without the former to is impossible to know the latter.

Our feet are standing within thy gates O Jerusalem - and they will never leave. This is Zionism, and the Untied

Gentiles call it 'racist' and debate how to take my city away from me. Foolish world; sooner will the sun fail to rise tomorrow. The Jews have come home to their Zion and have welded their city together with a fierce tightness that none least of all the humor that is the United Nations can sunder. A people which patiently bides its time for millennia will not easily - ever - give up its state and capital."

Rav Kahane's words reverberate. His books are being widely distributed and his ideas are reaching farther than expected. Jews, who would otherwise vote for Likud, are now attracted to Kach. Rabbi Kahane's ideology has no appeal to the Jews of the left, so in reality Kach does not represent a threat to the Labor party. It is in the Likud's immediate interest to stop Rabbi Kahane on his tracks or risk losing the greater part of its constituency. But Rabbi Kahane's choice of words sometimes paints him as an extremist. He now threatens to destabilize the entire system of government and demands fierce and violent action against Arab terrorists and rioters.

"If you love your people, you must hate Arabs, and not because they're Arabs, but because they're enemies. Even if those who hate you are Chinese, you hate those who hate you - unless you're crazy or stupid. Know this, that they are your enemies and they don't love you, and just as they will have no mercy on you, have no mercy on them. Thus said HaKadosh Baruch Hu (God): *go out against them as enemies. Just as they do not have any mercy on you, do not have any mercy on them*."

Rabbi Kahane's public appearances and publications continue to wake Jews up. The Likud is estimated to be reduced by half in the following elections if they fail to take action against the Kach party. Moreover, the world powers are also not pleased with Rabbi Kahane's propositions. In 1986, through illegal maneuvering Kach is declared to be a racist party by the Israeli judicial system and banned from running for the Knesset. It does not matter that members of Kach are Ethiopians, Moroccans, Yemnites, together with Europeans, American immigrants and natural born Israelis. What's more, followers of Rabbi Kahane span the religious gamut, from atheists to ultra-orthodox and everything in between. The only commonality among Rabbi Kahane's followers is a deep seeded love of Israel and the certainty that the Arab enemy must be expelled.

However, the ideology is considered extremist and the Likud uses illegal means to get rid of its competition, and it does so with the support of both Israel's left and the international community. It is not a matter of what is better for Israel, but how can the current political powers maintain their control over the country in spite of Arab aggression and popular discontent.

In 1988 both Israeli Arabs and those living in the 'disputed territories' (West Bank and Gaza) realizing that Kahane is no longer a threat, begin rioting and demanding Israel give them autonomy. The PLO for the first time, demands to be allowed to create an autonomous state of their own, one within Israel's sovereign borders. Due to the poor living conditions of many of these Arabs -still under the label of refugees, and perpetuated purposely by the Arab nations- they are portrayed to the world community as being victims and underdogs. This results in an unforeseen effort of the world community in pressuring Israel into compliance.

Threats of severe economic boycotts and the willingness to transform Israel into a pariah state creates panic among Israeli politicians. Since Israel is not yet self-sufficient and it depends on trade and commerce for its continued existence, Israeli diplomats (focused mainly in finances and not so much on survival) begin making the 'Palestinian' dream a reality. Palestinians embark on a tougher campaign of terror with the sole objective of pressuring Israel into compliance.

Rabbi Kahane's party is declared illegal, however, he vows not to stop campaigning, and continues to disseminate his ideas both in Israel and abroad. Rabbi Meir Kahane travels to America to both fundraise and increase awareness of the need to support Israel. One night in Manhattan in a New York City hotel, after concluding a speech calling on American Jews to immigrate to Israel, an Arab, disguised as an orthodox Jew, shoots Rabbi Kahane mortally wounding him. On November 5th 1990 Rabbi Kahane is assassinated.

Rav Kahane's assassination becomes a source of conflicting accounts. Nosair Al-Sayid who pulled the trigger is a member of Al-Qaeda, a then relatively unknown terrorist group. Rabbi Kahane's demise is timely and convenient especially for the members of the Likud who even after banning his political party continued to lose followers to the Rabbi's camp.

Sayid is thought by many to have been a mole for both the CIA and the Mossad (Israel's secret service). Sayid is not charged with murder after killing Rabbi Kahane in front of 300 people. He is captured a few blocks from the murder scene after a police shoot-out. Later that night, police arrive at Sayid's house and find two Middle Eastern men there: Mahmud Abouhalima and Mohammed Salameh. They are taken in for questioning. Additionally, police collect a total of 47 boxes of evidence from Sayid's house, including thousands of rounds of ammunition, documents in Arabic containing bomb making formulas, maps and drawings of New York City landmarks such as the World Trade Center; and details of an Islamic militant cell with mentions of the term "al-Qaeda," a relatively unknown group at the time.

Furthermore, they find recorded sermons by Sheikh Omar Abdul-Rahman, an Egyptian militant cleric, in which he encourages his followers to "destroy the edifices of capitalism" and destroy "the enemies of Allah" by "destroying their... high world buildings." Also found are tape-recorded phone conversations of Sayid reporting to Abdul-Rahman about paramilitary training, and even discussing bomb-making manuals. Videotaped talks of one Ali Mohamed delivered at the John F. Kennedy Special Warfare Center at Fort Bragg, North Carolina. Top-secret manuals also from Fort Bragg and even classified documents belonging to the US Joint Chiefs of Staff and the Commander in Chief of the Army's Central Command.

Ignoring all of this evidence, later that evening, Joseph Borelli, the New York police department's chief detective, publicly declares the assassination of Rabbi Kahane, the work of a "lone deranged gunman." He further states, "I'm strongly convinced that he acted alone... He didn't seem to be part of a conspiracy or any terrorist organization."

Investigators continue to ignore all evidence that suggests Sayid had not acted alone. District Attorney Robert Morgenthau, who prosecutes the case, later speculates that the CIA might have encouraged the FBI not to pursue any other leads. Sayid, it was later found, worked at the Al-Kifah Refugee Center, which is closely tied to covert CIA operations in Afghanistan. Although the CIA and the Israeli Mossad have always worked together, and it is clearly in the interest of many Israeli politicians to end Rabbi Kahane's career permanently, no evidence of a conspiracy becomes public.

Rabbi Kahane's murder strengthens Likud's position, but the world powers are siding ever more with the 'Palestinian' cause. Prime Minister Yitzhak Shamir responds to world pressure by agreeing to meet the Palestinian representatives in what became known as the Madrid Talks of 1991. Shamir meets with Arab terrorists together with American and Russian representatives to discuss giving more autonomy to the Palestinians and begins the process of unilateral concessions and appeasement.

Being that the voice of opposition has been silenced, Shamir capitulates, folds, and sells Israel short.

Aftermath:

Sayid is acquitted of Rabbi Kahane's murder, though he is convicted of lesser charges. He denies his involvement with the CIA or Mossad. Abouhalima and Salameh are also released only to be later apprehended and convicted for participating in the 1993 bombing of the World Trade Center.

Yitzhak Shamir attends the Madrid Peace Talks which lead to the sham known as the Olso Peace Accords.

Yasser Arafat, the Egyptian-born arch-terrorist, signs the Oslo Accords with Prime Minister Yitzhak Rabin, and becomes the leader of the manufactured Palestinian Autonomy.

"Stop being afraid. There is no danger that these guns will be used against us. The purpose of this ammunition for the Palestinian police is to be used in their vigilant fight against the Hamas. They won't dream of using it against us, since they know very well that if they use these guns against us once, at that moment the Oslo Accord will be annulled and the IDF will return to all the places that have been given to them. The Oslo Accord, despite what the opposition claims, is not irrevocable." - Yitzchak Rabin

Thousands of Jews are murdered by Palestinian terrorists shortly after they are armed by Shimon Peres and Yitzhak Rabin. These Arab usurpers enjoy autonomy in areas within the State of Israel; areas that were given to them as part of those agreements.

To this day, Palestinians refuse to recognize Israel as a Jewish state and are yet to renounce their pledge to use violence as a means to obtain their desired goals.

Israel is yet to repair the damage of the poor judgment and criminal behavior of left-wing politicians, including those that hide under the guise of the Likud.

In Memoriam: Rabbi Meir Kahane zt"l

By Shifra Hoffman

The author, who worked closely with Rabbi Kahane for many years, shares little known memories and insights of the dauntless, ideological MK and leader of the Kach party on the 19th anniversary of his tragic murder.

In this generation of fleeting allegiance and loyalty, particularly in the realm of Jewish leadership, it seems inexplicable that today, years after the brutal murder of Rabbi Meir Kahane, he is still mourned by so many Jews throughout the world. The phrase coined so as to perpetuate his ideas as well as his memory is "Kahane tzadak" (Kahane was right [i.e. his predictions were correct]).

Having worked closely for more than two decades with this self-sacrificing Jewish leader, both in the United States and in Israel, I feel impelled, on the l9th anniversary of his murder, to relate a few little known insights about the man behind the headlines. Although demonized by both left- and right-wing Israeli governments for his prophetic warnings concerning the rise of Arab nationalism and the dire consequences of making concessions to these implacable enemies, Rabbi Kahane remained undaunted. In his view, the Torah was the only timely and relevant 'road map' for the Jewish people.

During his election campaign for the Knesset, despite an Israeli Court decision that obliged television and newspapers to cover him as they did all other candidates, these 'democratic media outlets' refused to do so. This compelled the Rabbi to travel to speak each day in communities throughout Israel, often returning late at night in a state of complete exhaustion. Against all odds, he was elected to the Knesset. And following his unexpected success began to use the Knesset podium to sponsor the exact legislation upon which he based his pre-election platform.

This, as we know, is an unusual phenomenon in Israel where once elected, politicians feel they have the right to diametrically change their policy.

Rabbi Kahane believed that the only solution that could prevent a repeat of the Holocaust "final solution" in the Jewish state is the separation of Arabs and Jews. To underscore his commitment to this belief, he announced that he would go to Um El-Fahm, a hotbed of Arab terrorists and their supporters, to suggest that they leave the Jewish State, offering them compensation for their property. This was despite the fact that Jews received nothing when they were 'transferred' from the homes in Arab lands that they had lived in for generations.

The reaction to Rabbi Kahane's first Knesset speech in which he presented this plan was hundreds of phone calls that I received, many of them from "closet Kahane supporters" (as he used to refer to those Jews that secretly held his views, but feared to openly express them), urging me to implore the new MK to "tone down his rhetoric and change his image", now that he was an official member of the Government of Israel.

Knowing what his answer would be, I nevertheless dutifully related their requests. "Change my image," he replied as an amused smile crossed his face. "I worked too long and too hard to present this image. I want the citizens of Israel to know I am the same Meir Kahane they voted for."

He then travelled to Um El-Fahm to deliver his message.

A lesser-known facet of the Rabbi's boundless ahavat yisrael, the overriding love and compassion for the Jewish people, was a special charity fund from which he distributed thousands of shekels to hundreds of poor and often hungry Jews who came to his door each week. Those Jews shed bitter tears at his funeral, lamenting, "Who will help us now that Rabbi Kahane is gone?" The Chassdei Meir Fund established in his memory currently enlists dedicated volunteers who continue to provide and deliver large cases of donated food to poverty stricken Jewish families.

A further tribute to the Rabbi's influence can be found today in the hearts and minds of the young courageous Jews in Israel, who make their homes in caravans on the hilltops of the Land of Israel, and who, at great personal sacrifice, defend the right of Jews to settle anywhere in our G-D given homeland.

There are countless tales that deserve to be told about the life of this noble Jew, the personification of the Jewish scholar-warrior in the tradition of the Biblical King David.

However, the legacy that Rabbi Meir Kahane left the Jewish people and the world are his penetrating, insightful thoughts, expressed in the many popular books he authored. Among them are:

- Never Again

- Why Be Jewish?

- Uncomfortable Questions for Comfortable Jews

- Our Challenge

- They Must Go

- The Story of the Jewish Defense League

- Forty Years

And his magnum opus written shortly before his murder by an Arab terrorist:

- The Jewish Idea

In one of the volumes he signed for me personally, is an inscription I treasure dearly:

"In every generation, there are always a few who understand; Always understand... even if you remain among the few."

With Love of Israel,

Shifra

Shifra Hoffman is a journalist, Founder of the VICTIMS OF ARAB TERROR INTERNATIONAL ORGANIZATION (VAT) and Executive Director of SHUVA (Return) the Israel Emergency Aliyah Movement.

ZE'EV SHEMER

"Only liberals think
you can buy an Arab's dignity
with an indoor toilet."

"The modesty of holiness is contemptuously abandoned
and the nation wallows
in the nakedness of gentile culture."

"And I am afraid, for the first time,
that we are in the hands of people so blind and so mad
and so un-Jewish that we may not be able,
G-d forbid, to avert the catastrophe."

RMK

DEAR WORLD

By Rabbi Meir Kahane

November 1988

Dear World,

It appears that you are hard to please. I understand that you are upset over us, here in Israel. Indeed, it appears that you are quite upset, even angry and outraged! Indeed, every few years you seem to become upset over us. Today, it is the brutal repression of the Palestinians. Yesterday it was Lebanon; before that it was the bombing of the nuclear reactor in Baghdad and the Yom Kippur War campaign.

It appears that Jews, who triumph and who, therefore, live, upset you most extraordinarily. Of course, dear world, long before there was an Israel, we, the Jewish people - upset you.

We upset a German people who elected a Hitler and we upset an Austrian people who cheered his entry into Vienna and we upset a whole slew of Slavic nations - Poles, Slovaks, Lithuanians, Ukrainians, Russians, Hungarians, Rumanians. And we go back a long, long way in the history of world upset.

We upset the Cossacks of Chmielnicki who massacred tens of thousands of us in 1648-49; we upset the Crusaders who, on their way to liberate the Holy Land, were so upset at Jews that they slaughtered untold numbers of us. We upset, for centuries, a Roman Catholic Church that did its best to define our relationship through Inquisitions. And we upset the archenemy of the Church, Martin Luther, who, in his call to burn the synagogues and the Jews within them, showed an admirable Christian ecumenical spirit.

It is because we became so upset over upsetting you, dear world, that we decided to leave you - in a manner of speaking - and establish a Jewish State. The reasoning is that living in close contact with you, as resident-strangers in the various countries that comprise you, we upset you, irritate you, disturb you.

What better notion, then, than to leave you and thus love you - and have you love us? And so we decided to come home - to the same homeland from which we were driven out 1,900 years earlier by a Roman world that, apparently, we also upset.

Alas, dear world, it appears that you are hard to please. Having left you and your Pogroms and Inquisitions and Crusades and Holocausts, having taken our leave of the general world to live alone in our own little state - we continue to upset you.

You are upset that we repress the poor Palestinians. You are deeply angered over the fact that we do not give up the lands of 1967, which are clearly the obstacle to peace in the Middle East.

Moscow is upset and Washington is upset.

The Arabs are upset and the gentle Egyptian moderates are upset.

Well, dear world, consider the reaction of a normal Jew from Israel. In 1920, 1921 and 1929, there were no territories of 1967 to impede peace between Jews and Arabs.

Indeed, there was no Jewish State to upset anybody. Nevertheless, the same oppressed and repressed Palestinians slaughtered hundreds of Jews in Jerusalem, Jaffa, Safed and Hebron. Indeed, 67 Jews were slaughtered one day in Hebron - in 1929.

Dear World, why did the Arabs - the Palestinians — massacre 67 Jews in one day in 1929? Could it have been their anger over Israeli aggression in 1967? And why were 510 Jewish men, women and children slaughtered in Arab riots in 1936-39? Is it because of Arab upset over 1967?

And when you, World, proposed a U.N. Partition Plan in 1947 that would have created a Palestinian State alongside a tiny Israel and the Arabs cried and went to war and killed 6,000 Jews - was that upset stomach caused by the aggression of 1967? And, by the way, dear world, why did we not hear your cry of upset then?

The poor Palestinians who today kill Jews with explosives and firebombs and stones are part of the same people who - when they had all the territories they now demand be given them for their state - attempted to drive the Jewish State into the sea. The same twisted faces, the same hate, the same cry of "idbah-al-yahud" - "Slaughter the Jews!" that we hear and see today, were seen and heard then. The same people, the same dream - destroy Israel. What they failed to do yesterday, they dream of today - but we should not "repress" them.

Dear World, you stood by the Holocaust and you stood by in 1948 as seven states launched a war that the Arab League proudly compared to the Mongol massacres.

You stood by in 1967 as Nasser, wildly cheered by wild mobs in every Arab capital in the world, vowed to drive the Jews into the sea. And you would stand by tomorrow if Israel were facing extinction. And since we know that the Arab-Palestinians daily dream of that extinction, we will do everything possible to remain alive in our own land. If that bothers you, dear world, well - think of how many times in the past you bothered us. In any event, dear world, if you are bothered by us, here is one Jew in Israel who could not care less.

Rabbi Meir Kahane zt"l (1932 -1990)

ABOUT THE AUTHOR

Dr. Ze'ev Shemer is an academic English and social studies currently teaching on behalf of Bar Ilan University at colleges in northern Israel. He is the author of *Israel and the Palestinian nightmare*, and *The Answer*. Dr. Shemer specializes in middle eastern studies, Zionism, and comparative religion.